AH-CHOO! Sally covers her mouth
when she sneezes. What should she
do next?

Sally needs to wash her hands.
Staying clean helps keep us **healthy.**

Germs can spread when you sneeze. Washing your hands will help to stop the germs from getting into your body.

Germs get on your hands when you sneeze. These germs can spread on to your toys when you touch them. Then the germs can get on other people.

The germs can make other people
ill. Keeping your hands clean
helps everyone to stay healthy.

When should you wash your hands?
Wash your hands before you eat.
Wash your hands after going to
the toilet.

Wash your hands after playing outside. Wash your hands after touching animals.

Wash your hands when they look dirty.
Make sure the other people in your
family wash their hands too.

How do we wash our hands? Use warm water and soap. Rub your **palms** together to make lots of bubbles.

Rub the top of your hands. Rub between your fingers. Don't forget your nails and your wrists!

Rinse your hands with water. Dry your hands well with a towel. Germs love warm, wet places!

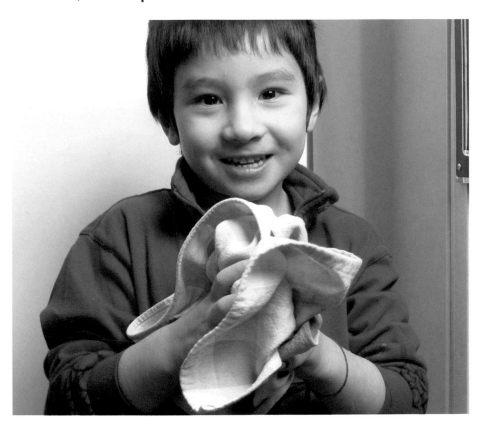

OUCH! Josh fell off his bike and grazed his knee. What should he do?
Josh asks an adult to clean his knee and put a plaster on it.

It's important
to keep cuts
and grazes
clean. If dirt
and germs get
into a cut it
could become
infected.

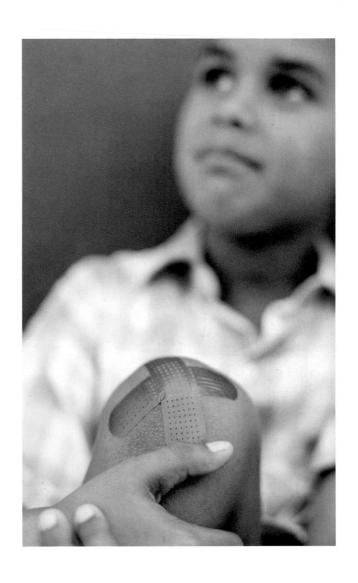

Rub-a-dub-dub! Billy likes to have a bath. Baths keep him clean and healthy. Baths and showers clean the germs and dirt off our bodies.

Don't forget to wash your hair!
We need to keep our hair clean to
stay healthy.

PEE-EEW! You might start to smell if
you forget to have a bath. Baths help
us to smell nice.

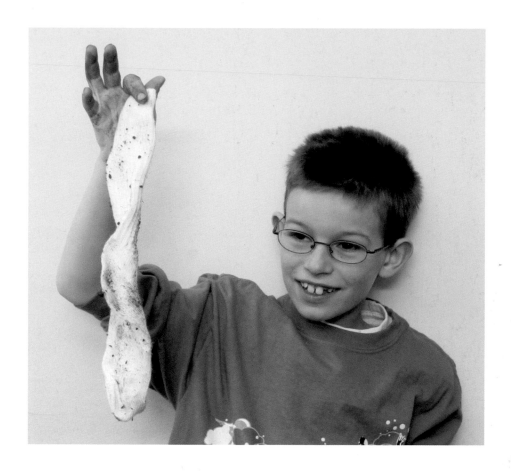

It's time to get dressed! Remember to
put on clean clothes. Dirty clothes
can start to smell. They are also
covered with germs.

People like to wear hats. You should keep your hat clean and not share it with friends. Germs and tiny insects called **lice** could get into your hat.

Lice make your head very itchy. They are also hard to get rid of. Never share hats, brushes, combs or anything that touches your head!

Brushing our teeth keeps us healthy too.

Germs and food can get stuck in our teeth and make holes in them. These holes are called **cavities.** OUCH! Cavities can hurt!

Sarah brushes her teeth in the morning and before she goes to bed. She uses a little toothpaste and brushes gently.

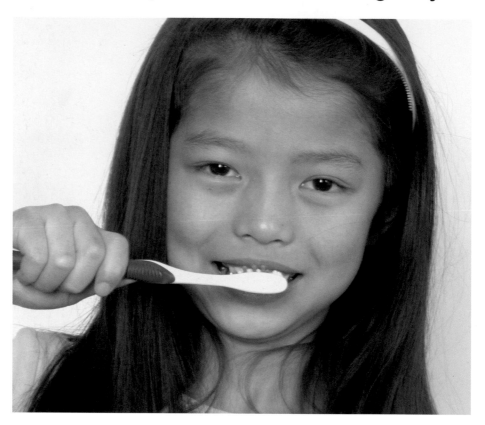

She brushes her tongue too. This gets rid of germs and gives her good breath.

Staying clean makes us feel good.
Washing hands, keeping cuts clean,
having baths and brushing teeth help
keep germs out of our bodies.

Doing all of these things helps to stop
us getting ill. Staying clean keeps
us healthy.

Let's Brush Our Teeth!

- Molly brushes her teeth every day. She brushes them in the morning. She brushes them before she goes to bed. She brushes them after she eats.

- Molly has a soft toothbrush. It's smaller than the one her older sister has. Molly's toothbrush is just the right size for her mouth and teeth. She will use her toothbrush for about three months. Then she'll get a new one.

- Molly gets her toothbrush wet so its bristles are softer. She puts some toothpaste on her brush. She only needs a small drop about the size of a pea.

- Molly starts to brush her teeth. She moves her toothbrush in tiny circles on the front of her teeth and near her gums. She brushes the back of her teeth in the same way. Next Molly brushes the top of her teeth. She moves her toothbrush back and forth.

■ Molly sings a song in her head as she brushes. That way she knows she has brushed for long enough. She needs to brush her teeth for about three minutes to get them clean.

■ She brushes her tongue too! This will give her fresh breath. Brushing her tongue will also get rid of germs called bacteria. **Bacteria** can cause cavities.

■ Finally Molly uses **floss**. She moves the string up and down between her teeth and gums. Her dentist showed her how to do this. Flossing can help reach the food stuck between her teeth.

■ Molly has finished brushing her teeth. Have you brushed your teeth today?

Books and Websites

Books

Llewellyn, Claire. *How To Stay Healthy* (I Know That!) Franklin Watts Ltd, 2005.

Rowan, Kate. *I Know How We Fight Germs* (Sam's Science) Walker Books Ltd, 2000.

Royston, Angela. *Why Does My Body Smell?: And Other Questions About Hygiene* (Body Matters) Heinemann, 2003.

Senker, Cath. *Keeping Clean* (Health Choices) Hodder Wayland, 2007.

Spilsbury, Louise. *Why Should I Wash My Body?: And Other Questions About Keeping Clean and Healthy* (Body Matters) Heinemann, 2003.

Websites

BBC Health: Kids' Health
http://www.bbc.co.uk/health/kids/

KidsHealth.org
http://www.kidshealth.org/kid/

Welltown
http://www.welltown.gov.uk/home/home_bathmenu.htm

Glossary

bacteria: germs that can cause cavities, sore throats and earaches

cavities: soft places or holes in your teeth that are caused by germs

floss: thin string that is used to clean between your teeth

germs: tiny living things that can make people sick

healthy: fit and well

infected: invaded by germs

lice: tiny insects that can get in your hair and make your head itch

palms: the flat part on the underside of your hands

Index

baths 16, 18

clothes 19–20, 21
cuts and grazes 14–15

dirt 10, 15, 16, 19

germs 5–7, 13, 15, 16,
   19, 20, 23, 25, 26, 29

hair 17

lice 20–21

sneezing 3, 5, 6

teeth 22–24, 28–29

washing hands 4–5,
   7–13

Photo Acknowledgements

The photographs in this book appear with the permission of: © White Packert/The Image Bank/Getty Images, front cover; © Todd Strand/Independent Picture Service, pp 3, 4, 8, 10, 18, 19, 23, 24, 25; © Image Source/SuperStock, pp 5, 7, 15; © The Photo Works/Photo Researchers, Inc., p 6; © Tom Myers, p 9; © Beth Johnson/Independent Picture Service, p 11; © Royalty-Free/CORBIS, p 12; © Brendan Curran/Independent Picture Service, p 13; © Francisco Cruz/SuperStock, p 14; Digital Vision Royalty Free, pp 16, 22, 26, 29; © Darama/CORBIS, p 17; © Laura Durman/Discovery Picture Library, p 20; © Sam Lund/Independent Picture Service, p 21; © PhotoDisc/Getty Images, p 27.